daily bread

harlem
river
press

Published for HARLEM RIVER PRESS by:
WRITERS AND READERS PUBLISHING, INC.
P.O. Box 461, Village Station
New York, NY 10014

Copyright © 1994 by Safiya Henderson-Holmes
Original Cover Art: Valerie Maynard
Cover Design: Terrie Dunkelberger
Book Design: Daryl Long, Terrie Dunkelberger

This book is sold subject to the condition that it shall not, by way of trade or otherwise, be lent, re-sold, hired out, or otherwise circulated without the publisher's prior consent in any form of binding or cover other than that in which it is published and without a similar condition being imposed on the subsequent purchaser.

All rights reserved. No part of this publication may be reproduced, stored in a retrieval system, or transmitted, in any form or by any means, electronic, mechanical, photocopying, recording, or otherwise, without prior permission of the publisher.

Copyright © 1994 by Writers and Readers Publishing, Inc.

ISBN Cloth 0-86316-310-6
ISBN Trade 0-86316-311-4
1 2 3 4 5 6 7 8 9 0

Manufactured in the United States of America

"...FOR, WHILE THE TALE OF HOW WE SUFFER, AND HOW WE ARE DELIGHTED, AND HOW WE MAY TRIUMPH IS NEVER NEW, IT ALWAYS MUST BE HEARD. THERE ISN'T ANY OTHER TALE TO TELL, IT'S THE ONLY LIGHT WE'VE GOT IN ALL THIS DARKNESS."

JAMES BALDWIN: "SONNY'S BLUES"

other books by author:

madness and a bit of hope.

daily bread

·

poems by
safiya henderson-holmes

HARLEM RIVER PRESS
NEW YORK • LONDON

dedicated:
to mama: esther henderson-brown
to daddy: chet otis lee henderson
to daughter: naimah lateefah holmes
to brother: walter edward dix
to brother: william flonoy chet henderson the 2nd
to brother: andre manzel chet henderson the 3rd
to life force: marvel cooke

contents

one

precision	2
food	3
force	5
witnessing a statement #3	6
life	8
love	10
birth defects #3	11
my first riot: bronx nyc 1962	13
to hell and back, with cake	15
speculations: the case of wanda webb holloway	18
witnessing a statement #5	22
gold by any means necessary	25
from 194,000 and counting	27
a news spot	29

two

1670 seward avenue	32
winter's remedy #3	34
february 16th 1990	35
driving (for mo and me)	39
letting go	41
sending rapunzel and juliet home	42
journey: for kathy and vivian	44
medium	47
small wonders	48

playing for our lives	50
amen	51
ace	52
james baldwin: presente	54
that day	57
all the wars for daily bread	58
falling in love	61
where to look for black love	62

three

marvel: for marvel cooke	64
1st draft	65
mergence	67
one size ain't all	69
a girl and her doll	71
shelter	73
divorce	74
abide #1	75
abide #2	76
a man and his doll	77
barbie out of the box	79
vows	81
why i like being called baby	82
peace #2	83

one

precision

war begins, clockwork:
short arm holds gun, long
arms tells short arm how
and where to aim gun.
third arm: malnourished, deformed
runs hysterically around the
entire world.

food

she come into store she come in
she come in with friends she come in with
nobody she bigger than me but she a girl she not
a woman but she talk like a woman she talk like a big-
woman
very bigger than me she drink the juice in my
store she drink the orange juice in my store
i have many family many women many more girls but
my women my girls are small they are small for a very
long time and they don't go many places by themselves
they stay very close to home they stay hidden in
places they stay until they are old and tired of hiding
but she she is so big for a girl her voice and her
mouth big and she say she can drink her juice i say
she steal it she say she didn't steal it i say she
steal it because i see her bigness i don't see her
smallness i see her loudness i don't see her quiet i
see her bigger than me i don't see her small young
i see she can hurt me if she's bigger she can hurt
and steal from me and yes her color makes her bigger
her black makes her bigger and stronger and she can hurt
me everybody know everybody say this not only
me or my kind but all kinds say this about her kind
and she say she doesn't steal juice and she say she
doesn't have to prove anything to me and i know girls
must prove everything girls and women must prove everything
everyday we must never stop trying to prove we will

food

die trying to prove and become big and unhidden but she
say no she doesn't have to prove anything and she's a girl
young her bones are still soft in places and her flesh
is tight and smooth and she say she doesn't steal and
she turn her head and flesh from me and she walks away
like a big big woman, no like a big big man and i am afraid
of bigness and men and i have a gun and i take the gun
from its safe hole and i hold the gun in the air and i see
her black hair and head and i shoot her and know that
this will teach her that she is little that she is girl
and will always have something to prove even with her dark
big color even with her dark big soul.

force

yes we watched the video a piece at a time slow
motioned regular and i saw how he just wouldn't
lie down he just kept gettin on up like he
was too big and too strong so they had to keep
beatin him til he just down like you got to break
horses and you got to break cattle and you got
to break bulls you keep on them with your force
til they can't see or hear nothing else and then you got
them where you want them and you can move them
the way you need to move them and they become
a part of you and they become like babies all loose
and soft and pliable and that's what had to be
done to him they had to get him that way look
how long his arms are look how long his legs are
how wide his back is my god somethin that big
comin at me i'd beat it a hundred times too
after the verdict i went on home my husband got
some beers and friends over the house they all
congratulating me and talkin 'bout all the hell
i been through then the company left and me and
my husband well you know i been away all that time
and so we ain't been too private for awhile and
we get in the bed and i'd done nearly forget how
heavy he was and his weight on me was so heavy
and so much i'm tryin to move under him and he's
gettin heavy on me you know pushin and i can
hardly breathe so i just go on and imagine that
he's the cop and i'm the black man and i stay down
and take it you betcha i stay down and take it.

witnessing a statement #3

okay, you people listen to me.
i came home, i'm moving around. it's normal. right?
can we agree on the normalcy of entering
your home and moving around? it's not female or male. it is.
i notice the bedroom window's open. no, i didn't enter
the bedroom first. is it female to enter the bedroom first?
i haven't a clue. i live there however the moments
strike me. no, i don't mean strike as in violence. i mean as
in an awakening. no i don't mean religion. i mean feeling,
sensing. no not metaphysically speaking. yes i meditate.

no, i'm not getting hysterical,
yes, i'm calm, fine. i went into the bedroom,
noticed the opened window, my stuff on the bed.
stuff? clothes, accessories. someone had been in my drawers.
am i making a joke? my stuff was on the bed.
am i making a joke? no i didn't leave the bedroom in a stir.
yes i knew what i was wearing to work. what does having
a large wardrobe have to do with anything?
yes i wear bikini underwear, sometimes i wear pajamas,
sometimes i sleep on my back, sometimes on my side,

sometimes i wear lipstick to bed. what are you asking?
yes my clothes are selected the night before.
yes i leave them over a chair, yes, the underwear's on top
sometimes near the window. but i don't use my underwear
as curtains. am i making a joke?

witnessing a statement #3

yes my underwear was visible to me
and yes someone was in my bedroom, rummaging my
stuff, they must've come through the window.
no, not because of my underwear and
yes i'm saying at that point i
didn't feel safe in my house. yes by point i mean moment,
and yes by point i mean knife, he stepped from the bedroom
closet and i saw he had a knife, and i saw that he meant
to rape me, yes i mean hurt me, no he didn't use the

knife, no he didn't touch me with the knife, no i don't assume
all men are here to rape me, yes i mean hurt, not with the knife.
how did i stop the knife? how does one stop a knife? i begged.
yes. i begged. no i didn't cry. yes i was scared. no i didn't cry.
how did i beg? i offered him my body for my life. yes as in flesh.
yes, as in mine. and yes i offered him a condom.
yes. i have condoms in my house. no, i'm not ready for sex.
yes, condoms are for sex. yes i offered him one as part of
my plea for my life. yes, if he was going to kill me, i wanted to live

and i wanted to protect myself. no i wasn't condoning.
i was protecting. yes he used it, yes he used it with
me. no i wasn't making love. i was being raped. i didn't consent,
i was saving my life. was there force? there's always force. did i
struggle?

i'm still struggling.

life

i seen the smoke and flames hell yeah i seen 'em
heard the shit on my radio and like
damn i was in the middle of the shit already and
i figured well hell this big fuckin truck can be used
like a tank if necessary 'cause this is the road for
me to go on home and i'm about gettin my ass home
and protectin my shit and hookin up with some buddies
if necessary ain't nobody stealin or burnin my shit
i see these black cats runnin up on the truck i
see them angry and shit but i'm pissed too and i stop
call them a few choice names you all know the names don't
give me the liberal act you all dressed in your suits
reportin the news like you ain't a part of it and you
like some kind surprised kid at their first horror movie
fuck that shit so yeah i called them those names now
i ain't my father i ain't my grandfather and i ain't my
great grandfather who probably had their great grandfather
hangin from a tree and stickin tar and chicken feathers
in his ass but i am a white man and i'm proud to be
a white man proud to be an american white man and i don't
see a damn thing wrong with that and yes i'm gonna drive
this truck up this motherfuckin burnin street and i'm
gonna tell anybody who got somethin to say about it to
kiss ass then i'm in the fuckin air and on the ground
i cursed every black son of a bitch i could see i'm
on the ground layin in my own blood somethin crashes
into my head my back i see myself standin over myself

life

my hair all twisted in my blood i'm fucked i hear voices
shoutin justice peace i see some more black cats run over
to me i can't push or shout them away everything in me
shouts nigga four black arms lift me my blood on their
shirts i smell their sweat and i hear a voice say easy my
man easy i whisper nigga again four black arms hold me
close carry me to a car drive through the fire to a hospital
stay til i'm washed clean and i'm sleep i dream about niggas
watchin me starin at me without blinkin or breathin.

love

called us savage beast murders inhuman mass
of destruction fuck that i know me and the me
i know was screamin louder than ever every incha me
roared felt like i had claws and teeth everywhere
not because i had become some kinda beast hell no
but because of all the animal things done to me
and people who look like me like man i don't
wanna hurt no more then this trucker come 'round
talkin much shit and i smell the shit you follow me
i taste it and i grab the sucka, grab the beast who's
been beatin me you hear what i'm sayin and he call
me one of the beast names and my flesh just crawls
all over him you know what i'm talkin about and there
ain't nothin but a whole buncha pain between us and
i just wanna run through all that war i just wanna
run through it and be gone and i hit that trucker
and i hit him and somethin in me say stop somethin
in me say go on somethin in me hold on to that
fool like for my life then i drop him there on
the ground by his truck and our blood drop him
like a last breath and i walk real slow on home
hear what i'm sayin i walk real slow on home get
there and stare for hours and hours at pictures
of my little girl i stare for hours.

birth defects #3

(when j.z. whispers
to himself)

uhm, uhm, uhm, uhm, uhm,
i,i,i,i,i, was, there
uhm, uhm, on the bed changin
her, changin, changin, her
i was watchin, i was watchin
her face and i touched her
chin and she was soft and
my finger felt her chin again
and she was still soft and smooth
and she smiled at me and she
and she touched my face near my
eye and lips and her fingers were
soft and i sucked her fingers
and her taste was good uhm, sweet
and tender and i felt special
and big and small and alone and
crowded and wet and dry and i
sucked her fingers and she laughed
and made soft sounds, my,my,my,my,
baaaaabeeee made soft sounds in my
ear and i swallowed somethin in my
throat and i hit somethin off the
back of my head and i heard somethin
fall in the room and i saw somethin
move in my eye and a, and a i,i,i,i
smelled her softness on her neck and she kicked
my chest and i heard somethin fall in the
room again and i saw somethin move in

birth defects #3

(when j.z. whispers
to himself)

my eye and i uhm rubbed my chest across
her belly and i rubbed my chest across
her thigh and somethin crawled up my
back and stabbed my neck and freeze me
over her and i was hard and scared
and my legs were not mine and my
baby was not mine but i saw wide
in front of me and she smelled safe
and clean and new and sweet and i
was so little and big and loud and
quiet and uhm, and uhm, and uhm i
rushed into her for safety, 'cause
she would hide me uhm, she would hide
me a long time.

my first riot: bronx nyc 1962

we are nine. two
boys and a girl,
walking home from
dracula's matinee.

in a vacant lot
we see smoke and
flame, run into
heat with our mouths

and eyes locked open.
find jarcaps and
cardboard to scoop
dirt and cover fire.

smokey the bear
taught us dousing
and smothering.
good citizens, we work

to save the unclaimed space.
somewhere in the smoke
we see and hear a man
shouting- hey you bastards-.

my first riot: bronx nyc1962

his pale face growing
larger in the smoke.
-you black bastards,
with your gadamn fires.

i'm calling the cops-.
i watch him run,
think of dracula
entering a grave, taste

ashes on my teeth.
-fuck him-, gerald
says, finds a small
flame, carries it to

a pile of sticks and
paper. it stretchs and
cracks the summer
we stare until our eyes

burn and the dirt is
hot and mean again.
sirens screech and howl
up our backs, we run

for our lives. blood racing,
vampires not far enough
away.

to hell and back, with cake

it's spring, saturday.
the small, soundview
bakery's stuffed,

but i'm the only kid.
the one black. i stand firmly
in front of cupcakes:

polite desserts in pleated paper
skirts and thick icing hats;
chocolate, vanilla, pistachio.

pure glaze. my allowance melts
in my pocket. i want two
vanilla and two chocolate.

i want the four in a bakery box,
separated by bakery tissue,
tied in red bakery string.

i want to walk home
with my special box
softly swaying in my hand.

after seven pies, two ice cream cakes
a dozen blueberry muffins, fudge
and three pounds of mixed cookies,

to hell and back, with cake

i'm next. i lay a steamy finger
on the bakery glass.
-two chocolate and two vanilla please-.

the woman behind the counter's
new to neighborhood and bakery.
her apron loosely tied

and still unfolding, fresh
creases dodge flour and syrup spills.
she doesn't know my name,

or notice how each week
i grow an inch higher than
the counter, no inquiry into

my parents' health or pastry
needs. she holds her arms across
her chest as shield, patrols

the cupcakes. her blue eyes,
darts. she looks at cupcakes
and maims them. -we don't have

what you want. got white
cupcakes or black cupcakes.
what you want is some place else-

to hell and back, with cake

my finger's a plug in the bakery dam,
save the bakery from the flood of gawks,
drowning the sugary good. my finger stays

on the glass. the color leaving the tip.
my coins growing stones. -i want two
chocolates and two vanilla- i say

cupcakes. i say please.
she cocks, aims. -we got white,
we got black. that's it,

you take that or you go on.-
the cupcakes are dead, the pies, cookies,
fudge dead in their gaze.

i remove my finger from the glass.
my coins and i pallbearers
of late sweetness.

we carry it out the bakery door.
other mourners alive,
but holding their breath.

speculations:
the case of wanda webb holloway

> channelview texas, march 15th 1991
> "channelview texas, march 15th - the azaleas
> and jasmines have bloomed across the sterling
> green subdivision here, and in two nearly
> identical houses around the corner from each
> other, two mothers have resumed their routines
> of car pools and trips to the mall.
>
> they show no signs that they are the suspect
> and intended victim of a purported murder plot
> born of big envies and small ambitions."
>
> new york times
> sunday march 17th 1991

azalea and jasmine blooming:

she's a white american, christian,
believer in god and her home town.
she plays the church organ, attends
church several days a week. she lives
in texas, in the suburbs on a plot
of weekly cut grass, within the wooden

frame of a small, neatly painted house.
no garbage anywhere. she's a decent woman,
believes in sit-to-table dinners, easy-
walking shoes, somber colors, a few
select pastels for spring. her make-up
isn't too much for her age or her desires.

speculations:

the case of wanda webb holloway

her desire: to see her thirteen year old
daughter on the cheerleading squad of her
home town highschool. a tiny thing to wish
for in the bigness of texas. a big thing
to wish for in the smallness of love.
she and her daughter are not blondes.

they've had as much fun in their
lives as god and money has allowed.
wanda irons her own clothes, washes
delicates by hand, her undergarments
soak and rinse twice, dry in private places
away from sun and neighbors.

wanda sweeps her own floors, dusts
and polishes her own furniture, removes
a season's sludge from her own windows.
and yes, she has a couple of precious
pieces: a pair of diamond earrings
she's willing to barter for her cheerleading

speculations:

the case of wanda webb holloway

dream. a pair of diamond earrings
in exchange for life, in exchange for
a breath above the rest. of course she
isn't rich. savings are for distant futures,
disappearing dreams. wanda holds her
diamond earrings in a fist between her
breast, in spit between her teeth,
in sweat between her legs. a pair
of diamond earrings in exchange for life,
in exchange for the life of another
channelview mother with cheerleading dreams
of her own, batons and pom-poms

on the dinner table, on the coffee table
alongside a cold beer, on the bed as she
kneels to pray and beg her soul to keep,
for her sin to be lesson not a curse.
wanda called on god and anyone in need
of diamond earrings, anyone in greed

for diamonds, anyone who will take
this treasure and her one desire and
load them into a gun's barrel, or onto
the end of dynamite, or into the gone-
wild engine of a mad hit-and-run car,
take these pressurized dreams and do

speculations:

the case of wanda webb holloway

away with the nightmare of competition
and the cancerous sweat of losing.
what else are diamonds for?
to anyone wanda will release her fist
and the name of the other mother,
address of the other neatly painted house,

the color and size of that other baton.
what else are desires for?
mother love. priceless mother love.
will we all go insane for our children,
will we all go so sweetly insane?

witnessing a statement #5

dear women:

who was i before the harassing
questions, abusive cameras,
and the rows of suited white men
who wanted to know patterns
of my pussy, not my brain.
did you know me, what name
or names did you call me,
where in your memory
or your forgetfulness did my
ambitious coloredness live,
and how did i live there, alone
or in the world, starving or eating
from your mouth?

for your own needs you found
me, not as me, but as you.
i was climbing an eternal ladder,
at what rung i hung from didn't matter.
each slippery with lies. my own
and a system of other. i only knew
i didn't want to fall. however far the top,
there are too many deaths beneath me.

and no, i didn't call you sister
until i needed you. and you the same.

witnessing a statement #5

you don't know my mother,
or the dirt she's turned and seeded.
nor do i know yours. we've both denied
and dyed our roots for some god's sake.
but this too doesn't matter. only a
circumstance of femaleness
brings us into this one glaring room,
not an invitation to dinner, or a party,
not a visit home. but there you raise my fist
as if it's yours or ours. shake this fist
in the faces of your enemies and lovers,
shouting for them to see us bound and
bleeding.

and the cameras ram down your throat.
aim at your words, trustfully following
the echoes of my life. in these split media
frames it appears to everyone, even the rows
of suited white men that our nerves run
together, synapse and charge towards
and away from whatever there is to fear.
focused in the small, eyes of cameras
without the blur of dream or wishing,
we are one big, pure action: smooth,
swift as the shutter of a lens.
a picture of a family.

witnessing a statement #5

but when these cameras and questions
return my body and tongue to the dark,
to that crowded ladder of knees and spines,
this moment dimmed and muted,
this room another shadow on our faces,
your words kicking into the blackness.
will we call each other sister? will our nerves
meet in the muscle of our hearts, rush again
to a central opening, where our lives contract
and release a family picture of ourselves,
re-member and claim every woman in it:
this aunt, that daughter, this niece, that wife,
this friend, that bitch brave, powerful,

unafraid?

gold by any means necessary
(for my brother and his first false arrest)

what is it
to walk into
a store casually,
with your hands
in your pockets
and full leisure
on your face,
what is consumer
in this posture,
what is thief,
what is black
in this posture,
what is hidden
what is inscribed?

what happens
to a black male
as he grows from
boy to man,
from shadow,
to lurking,
from handholding
to handcuffs
as he enters,
walks to a gold
jewelry counter
and admires
a pair of expensive
earrings?

gold by any means necessary

-too long, too hard-
the store police say.
-for my mother's birthday-
he says, soberly,
showing his cash,
a college i.d.,
office keys
as they push him into a room,
slam the door.
why isn't he believed,
what isn't being believed;
his money, his birth,
his caring, or his lack of rage?

from 194,000 and counting

dear mom america;

this isn't a letter to ask how you
are doing. i no longer give a damn.
this is a letter to curse you out,
disown you, as you've disowned me.
for nearly ten years i've been telling you i'm dying,
in your hospital bed, under your thin sheets,
thick with fever and accusing stares.
the room's decked in your favorite colors:
opaque hellos and pale regrets.

but you don't visit. i can't shout through the hole
your underpaid attendants have pierced in my neck,
your tubes choke me with all your rules
of who i am, who i am to love.
your regard heavier than a lover's grief.
but what do you know about my love or grief?
what do you know of my lips which held your name,
the skin now lifting in tiny shards cutting
my tongue whenever i speak?
every word said about you or me

seeps into the crevice of my mouth and rots,
infecting me further; giving you more reasons
for absence and silence. i've been told how you
draw pictures of me, trying to capture your ideas
of men and strength. but what do you know
about my strength?

from 194,000 and counting

the power of my chest as it refuses
to collapse in your malignant air?
each lung heaving you
into the hollowness of your heart.
what do you know about hearts?
my own: a coal burning furnace.
my desire to live beyond your prognosis:
the miner shoveling without exhaustion
but with no hope of relief.
the miner's sweat carving rivers in my bony back.
what do you know about my bones?:
floating in the circles of this bed, in the circles
of costs for cure and costs for bombs,
floating in your luminous shame.

but what do you know about shame?
i was your child, holding your hand.
but then, what do you
know about children?
their palm prints: the wrinkles
in your face.

a news spot

"berlin, nov 4th- a scandal
over charges that a german
company distributed AIDS-
infected blood, perhaps knowingly,
to dozens of hospitals is spreading
anxiety throughout germany,
and today spilled over into
other european countries where
hospitals also bought blood
from the accused company.

italy, sweden, france, switzerland
and australia today halted the sale
of blood products purchased from the
company, UB Plasma, officials in
britain, greece and the czech republic
launched intensive searches to see
if any of the potentially tainted
products were stored in their hospitals.

a news spot

german health administrators held
an emergency meeting in hamburg
today, and estimated afterward that
about two million germans have received
blood products at hospitals which were
customers of UB Plasma.

some german newspapers have put
the number as high as 15 million.

>   the new york times
>   new york, friday,
>   november 5th 1993

two

1670 seward avenue
(apt. 7g bronx nyc)

in nearly every dream
i'm that apartment in the bronx:
six rooms, seventh floor,
corner, left of elevator.

see me: narrow foyer where
mama shakes her hands for
daddy not to drink. booze
never hidden in the kitchen.

kitchen white and yellow,
semi-glossed with daddy's
promises of sobriety.
sobriety in a pile of wishbones

over kitchen sink.
see me: father john and
asafetida, wheat germ, cod liver
oil, milk of magnesia and ginger
roots in medicine drawer near stove.

stove burning cookies.
smoke falling out the window.
window open. mama screaming
in the openness, her back bending

1670 seward avenue
(apt. 7g bronx nyc)

on edge. see me: edge of daddy's
skin as he trembles and pulls mama
into his chest. her hands slapping
daddy's face until it rains.

see me: rain and ice on bottom
of mama's boots as she stands at
front door and locks it, says
-we're moving, leaving forever-

see me: forever at that apartment
door, seeping into floor, brick,
stone.

winter's remedy #3

i've buried much
under the frozen

flesh of syracuse:
desire.

conversations
with spring frighten me.

february 16th 1990:

(one day when we were weak)

i'm sitting in a hospital room
with my oldest brother and
a psychiatrist from india.

no. i'm running towards my
brother, running with the
lead legs of an escaped

slave, to free another.
every motion killing, my breath
and blood a map to this room,

my brother sits with his arms
folded, but bursting against them,
his sweat an armor, his tremors a weapon.

he's been fighting them
for days. -who are they?-
the psychiatrist wants to know.

a pen and triplets of yellow
paper held on an unshaking knee,
a statistical arsenal aimed

at my brother's gut. if only
a pen and reams of numbers
could stop them, line them up

february 16th 1990:
(one day when we were weak)

neatly and slash them with
our daily lives, our daily routines.
they live in my brother's gut,

above his groin where they rock
and laugh whenever my brother makes
love, whenever my brother tries

to escape into the lull of love
they taunt and tease in his navel.
my brother scratches them

until he comes or bleeds, and
the gush of come or blood is shadow
where my brother hides for a little while.

his black six foot five frame
fetal and warm and safe for a little
while. until they find him at a fruit

or newsstand, or at his manhattan
apartment door and they've jerked
with the key and colors of his room,

or placed the faces of unfamiliar
people in his mirror, or in the
palms of his hands, and he'd wash

february 16th 1990:
(one day when we were weak)

until he heard weeping.
-your brother's suffering
from severe paranoid delusions,-

the psychiatrist says. his pen writes
a symphony for them:
-he must be admitted or medicated.

-he will become harmful
to himself or someone else.-
my brother's bulging eyes target

the doctor from india, a look charging
from a long, gray tunnel. spears,
whips and thorns of roses

in a blink. they're under the paint
of the hospital room, in the metal
and wood. -they'll find you too,-

my brother says, -it doesn't start
or stop with me, they're after every
one, other than themselves.

-your black's no whiter than mine.-
the doctor stands, writes, exits.
they crawl and chant around the words:

february 16th 1990:
(one day when we were weak)

-i'm sorry. but this is what we have.
i'll send in a nurse to talk with you.-
my brother's skin is on patrol,

soon it will leap in full war attack.
and i'm his point guard,
the remains of his army.

here they come.
here we are.
our tremors and sweat:

bullets in the walls.
our tremors and sweat
dream splitting bullets

in the walls.
aiming, i try to remember
how to spell my mother's

maiden name.

driving

(for mo and me)

though the routes of
our birth were different,
we are sisters, here on the same road,
heading to who knows where.

i say north. you say south.
we chance it, and on foot.
at this big age no license
or car, or man with hands

or heart strong enough to
carry us. but would we allow
carrying? we were born of women
who walked alone.

we load our primordial backseats:
you with two daughters, me with one,
and books, names we call ex-lovers,
schemes to make money and sense.

on hills and blind turns
we always say girlfriend
we need a car: a black benz
with jacuzzi and a trunk of fine wine.

driving

(for mo and me)

we continue to climb, ease into turns.
at night, now and then, from exhaustion
or wonder we stop to see who, besides us,
is going this way.

you show your long dancer legs.
i lick my lips and wave.
do we wait; and those taillights
far ahead, do we run, leave all,

dash towards the red flash?
yes. no. combination of maybes and whynots.
old stop and go routines holding us
in neutral, disengaging us until

we kick ourselves into drive.
and then? we keep walking, keep feeding
the kids, keep studying, testing each other,
asking questions over and over

memorizing answers
until they disappear,
and we have pedal to floor.
our own red flash behind us.

letting go

my daughter's second day
at her new school bus stop alone:

an unfamiliar, half awake
syracuse corner, two endless blocks

from nine years of hand holding
across streets and bridges. my larger

and already endangered body
between her and everything else.

in her left coat pocket there's
a quarter to phone home:

if the bus is late, or never arrives,
or...

it's the unattached 'or' that freezes
me to the window, counting every child

on any corner, noting the color hat
or scarf, watching them wait for something

which will too soon be more than
a yellow bus whose doors open easily

and whose routes never change.

sending rapunzel and juliet home

in a rage for sameness
my daughter screamed herself
to sleep for doll-like tresses.

too many days of her seven years
were spun in dreams of rapunzel
hair and juliet locks around her

neck and heart. in my own rage
for sameness i threatened to cut her hair,
attack these dreams where they sleep.

scissors as gun. histories of denied
beauty the trigger. where to start
the killing? i sat at the foot of her bed,

hid my face under a veil of reason
and hurt. here thick braids rallied,
each with an eye and a stone;

even as prey incapable of laying
flat, presuming innocence or death.
were the scissors too small a weapon?

i remember my mama:
iron comb redhot in her hand,
redhot in my black woolly hair.

sending rapunzel and juliet home

the smoke of dying hair
a signal of saturday nights and
sunday mornings. burnt ears and necks,

offerings to gods not loving me,
or mama. forcing difference from our hair,
blessing us with pieces of worlds they didn't

want. what god am i, what pieces
of my daughter do i want. with this secret
shearing what worlds am i giving her?

her head turned. the braid above
her left ear unraveled, fanned out
in a V. i dropped the scissors,

kissed the spot of truce,
whispered into her spine-
rapunzel and juliet, please,

go home.-

journey: for kathy and vivian

1.
what to bring on long journeys
into ourselves, which years fold
neatly in fists, stack safely along
the spine, become invisible under
our tongues?

burdened with re-membering
and needs to remember more,
we never travel light. every breath
and blink necessary extras to load
and carry.

2.
two friends of mine, women,
one turk, one jew filled their
stomachs with their mothers' water
and went into the desert
of their hearts.

palestine

vivian had been to her vast dryness
before. the visit coated her tongue,
making her speechless. how did her heart
hold so many soldiers and bullets?
so many dead men floating through her lungs

like poisoned fish.

palestine.

journey: for kathy and vivian

loaves of bread burned in vivian's throat.
children pounded her ribs, moaned
in her armpits, eyes clung to her
neck, returning to new york
she flew out of her breast, names

of the wounded and hungry peeled
from her skin.

palestine

3.
kathy had never been within these nerves,
but had been awakened since girlhood
by sounds of approaching tanks, by whispers
of women as they ran from their sleep
into her dream.

kathy entered through the marrow
of her spine, where her great grandmother
sits sifting jewish laws and loves. kathy
entered slowly, climbing generations of spines.
climbing the steepest world: traitor.

when the pain was too great she bit
a picture of her daughter.

journey: for kathy and vivian

palestine

kathy collected daughters in her hair,
in the seams of her clothes, fed
them the lines in the palms of her hands.
returning to new york, she walked out of her
grandmother's fists, shook until every daughter

was freed.

palestine.
o, palestine.

medium

i watch an armless
sidewalk painter:

a woman, pastels
in neat rows at her feet.

ankles overused palettes.
new york city concrete her canvas.

she balances on one foot,
grips color with the other.

she concentrates on light
in painting's eye:

how much white?
i stand cautiously

near the painting's right hand.
shift my weight from leg to leg.

i concentrate on light
in painter's shoulders:

how much red?

small wonders

i'm a little girl.
i wear crinolins, bows,
laced ankle socks, t-strapped
shoes. but i'm also a bat:

small, brown, red eyes.
only bat in house.
mama and brothers sleep.
lights, radio, t.v. off.

i hover front door.
wait for daddy. i'm patient.
mama believes in me only
as her little girl.

in morning, mama rubs
cold cream on my elbows and knees,
fills my hair with barrettes,
starches my crinolin, irons my bows.

in night, when daddy enters
i fly to his ear, beg him
to step quietly. no whiskey
loud talk. no whiskey blind falls.

small wonders

i lead him to couch,
lay him on stomach,
search pockets for dollars,
cover his snores and smells

with his coat, go to my room,
hang between his sleep and mama's
until cold cream slips over my wings.

playing for our lives

my brothers and i
sometimes play
cops and robbers
when we're sad,

sometimes my brothers and i play
martians and school
when we're glad.

and sometimes,
when we're feeling
silly,

and want a little mischievous fun,

my brothers and i sneak into the kitchen
and pour daddy's
whiskey

into the sun.
o silly willies
giggle til
we cry.

pouring daddy's
whiskey
into the sky.

amen

every other month
on one sunday,

after god and nosy
neighbors, we'd go home

to dad's french toast.
cinammon unlocking

the door. he was
a french toast master:

six large eggs, one container
of milk, one loaf of wonder

bread, honey. he soaked
slices separately, fried

them in butter, wiped pan
clean for each new arrival.

he stacked his specialty
on a platter, carried it

in both hands, syrup tucked
under chin. he tightroped

to table. the stack high,
sweet. we didn't any

to fall.

ace

even now, whenever
i see a tennis court,
i don't walk by.

i stand, hod the fence,
put you on my side
of the net.: you're in

your red bermuda shorts
and yellow t-shirt, your
glasses held to your head

by a thick rubberband,
elastic supports on both wrists,
white sneakers, white socks,

sweat everywhere except
in the grip of your racket
and your ball. you like lob

with topspin, dart balls
across the net, all you see it that
left hand corner. daddy, i tell

everyone your fame,
before arthur ashe: how you
taught althea gibson tennis,

ace

how you gave paddle ball
to the bronx, how the
bronx named you a street.

tennis racket your weapons
slung across your shoulder,
loaded and ready for anyone's

court. if johnnny walker
and jack daniels were real men,
daring you at the net,

you would've aced them
ages ago. no volley.
six-love, six-love, six-love.

james baldwin: presente
(macdowell art colony, summer '92)

i hold you, on a cot
in a room where embers
of a man's love for men
and music simmer
and fire late into the night.

when this piece of earth
is blacker than you or me,
quieter than our first touch
of something white: this paper,
that face which promised pay.

james, here in the center
of a room, in the middle
of woods as a fox hunts
shadows for food, as heat
from a lamp warms my head

whenever i bend over you, pulling
edges of you into me, you make
me feel my nigger skin, whipped,
hung and left.
you shout at my breast. read!

as if i haven't taken in much,
even though after each book
i am bursting, chunks of me
hitting the white walls of every cabin
in this colony of art and artists

james baldwin: presente

(macdowell art colony, summer '92)

where you came to write
and smoke in an american
gazebo with a mountain and a star.
every morning i am spent
and smell of too much fucking.

after every book you pit
your tongue against my spine,
press my nerves open and flat,
search my breathing with your teeth
for julia, frank, tish, fonny, leo, ruth,

arthur, hall, sharon, giovanni, rufus.
make of my vertebrae the streets
where they lived, the streets that took them
head first. yes, fonnys are in jail.
yes rufus is jumping off that damn

bridge, yes the giovannis cruise
sidewalks of france and harlem,
rake their hearts raw with their lovers sighs
and yes sharons search for the truth.
and yes i am julia needing to be saved.

stimata ripe between my eyes.
mr. baldwin i want to fight you,
stab your pain with the ice pick
of my own, with the poisoned spear
of my daughter's as she enters her catholic

james baldwin: presente
(macdowell art colony, summer '92)

classroom, silently praying for the teacher
to see her and not see her,
hear her, and not hear her,
point to the god in her and swear
the gospel is not there. yes mr. charlie

swells with the blues. and yes
it's evident that things are not seen
or heard. but your pain seems bigger
than mine, than ours, as if you've taken
every door and world you wrote

yourself against, held yourself there
for the bull's eye or the donkey's ass,
moving only your eyes and spit.
in this lonely night, as moon manic
fox strips legs from a deer,

pages of your books are layers
of flesh, muscled, just above my
head. my clit has moved to the nape
of my neck where i tighten for you
word after word after word.

soon i will be able to tell
how long the train's been gone
but not why its gone so fare without
us.

that day

the day my father died:
i hadn't slept the night before.
my daughter hungrier than usual
sucked milk from my breast

and bones. we were awake and limp
when sun appeared. one breast
in her mouth, me pumping the
other.

when the phone rang and my
father's wife told me of his
passing, the breast in my daughter's
mouth swelled.

the one i pumped poured. my milk
gushed in two streams: one for my
daughter's life, one for my
father's.

all the wars for daily bread

during her first visit
to my upstate home mama and i
watch t.v.: soldiers deplane,
children waving small american flags
run towards war worn men.

in the corner of my eye, mama:
we haven't talked beyond chit-chat
in years, years of me growing
into just another woman,
years of her wishing i wouldn't,

monthly concerns of department store
bargains, an occasional glimpse
of something expensive.
without looking i watch mama.
she says -war's everywhere-

on television: a female soldier,
arms in casts as wide as ironing boards.
a male soldier on a stretcher, long stemmed
bouquets and one leg.
mama says -when will we learn?

it makes me angry.-
i focus on soldier with floral
prosthesis: tulips, roses, tiger lilies.
when the flowers wither,
how will he walk?

all the wars for daily bread

mama says -i'm sorry, i don't mean
any disrespect, but those soldiers
don't have a thing over me.
i've been in some kind of war all my life.-
i clean my fingernails, think of bombs

dropping on houses, on heads.
-it's hell- i say.- my hands feel heavy.
a familiar weight. impossible to lift
them in a coordinated arc,
land around mama's waist, hug her.

t.v. gives guns again, infernos bullets make.
when did i stop hugging mama?
her breast still larger than mine.
what of a bomb's shape?: as penis,
as breast, as daddy's fist in mama's back,

her body spilling into my bedroom,
my body taut as torpedo against my bedroom
door, daddy exploding on the other side.
what is 'peace? mornings of tentative
ceasefires, afternoons of playing chicken,

daring the silence for a walk in the park.
mama had studied piano and singing,
wanted to be ella fitzgerald
or sarah vaughn. she says,
-all those nights of fighting your father,

all the wars for daily bread

and getting up, acting like i won,
or worse, acting like i hadn't fought at all.
trying to keep the whole thing together.
you know. your father's dead. other one's dead too.
and the mess with my oldest and his family.

and dear daughter your mother's tired.
i want to push that soldier off that
stretcher and lay down myself.-
she laughs, rubs her skirt.
i watch soldiers smile for cameras

shoulder to shoulder. brothers.
i flash mama's face, blurred image
of my own marriage, my own battles:
conversations thrown as grenades,
unseen wounds of my daughter,

promises maimed and dying.
i want to call mama comrade,
captain, land in her lap,
both of us escaping, both of us alive.
the t.v. soldiers salute.

my arms lift, awkward, graceless.
mama's skirt: perhaps a clearing.

falling in love

mama, we were on the plane
returning from california. our first
vacation together. i sat near the window,
you next to me on the aisle, we talked
and ate slowly, wanting california to stay
in our bones, not leave with each exhale.

then the elderly woman across from you
stood, leaned into you, whispered to your ear.
white strands of her hair caressed yours.
you smiled. the dimple in your left cheek
which appears whenever you're surprised,
marked your amazement.

your hands went to the woman's waist,
reached for a long, brown belt hanging from
a loop. you carried the belt around her,
stopping at each loop, gliding your hand over
the skirts fabric. smoothed everything in place.
buckled the belt gently, as if fastening

the lock of a great secret chest.
the elderly woman held your hands
on her stomach. a tear avoided the dimple.
the elderly woman sat. the plane rose.
and i fell in love with you mama.
i fell in love with you, then and there.

i loosened my belt to consummate the desire.
the dimple stayed.

where to look for black love,

(a guide for the readers and believers of the
book, *the blackman's guide to understanding
the blackwoman*.):

look in a cotton fiber,
a peanut shell, in blood plasma,
in the blink of a traffic light,
at an aerial view of washington d.c.,
at the top of the north pole,
in a solo two-year sailing voyage
around the world, in the copper roofs
of blue mountain new york, in a cake
of soap, in the name of beatrice,
in the name of peas and rice,
in a shipyard in a san diego bay,
in the heat of a ball of iron, in a four
hundred meter dash, in the name
of jesse ownes, in the name of wilma
rudolph, on a baldwin page, in a hurtston
book, stroke a langston poem, whisper
the lines of a hansberry play, pray with
a catlett painting, give birth in the clay
of augusta savage, walking down the aisle
with handy's blues, suck a coltrane sax,
chew a fitzgerald scat, gulp a joplin bop,
ride a baptist wail, hear the testimony
of brer rabbit, get sanctified with fish fries,
lucky leaves and john the conquer roots,
wear a zoot suit, hussle 'till you twist,
mombo 'til you samba, marangue 'til
you grind, grind 'til you burst,
burst 'til you star.

THREE

marvel: for marvel cooke

you are my
old woman
in purple
and i wear
you always.
all ways.

1st draft

the first blood
i ever wished
for was a poet's:

thin, brown, chewing
pens and pain.
we had talked

words all day.
tried to find the
'just-rights' to give

to a moment he had
with an old woman
and a raw chicken.

the old woman had said,
-son, poorly as you is,
you better put on this

poultry and put off
that poetry.-
my friend was sixteen

and harmfully serious.
youthful follower of 'beat'
and 'howl'.

1st draft

he said, -good poetry needs
blood- stabbed his left palm
with his pen.

his blood bubbled, then hid.
he said, -it'll flow in a minute,
soon as the soreness sets in, it'll flow.-

i stared at my friend's
wounded hand, thought of the times
my daddy had said never

watch my hamsters give birth,
how the looking would make
the hamster crazy, and she'd eat

her young.
he stabbed his palm again.
we waited for blood and poem.

mergence

last night i dreamt
of myself as

a little girl:
fawn brown, spindly.

i sat beside
my grown woman

self in a group
of other grown

women fully
dressed in fashions

which did not give
for touching. my

selves were the only
naked ones. the

other women
watched our skin. i

whispered to my
self that i loved

myself girl-like,
delicate as

mergence

i still appeared
to be. my girl-

like rested her
head on my breast.

i felt her tongue.
i carried girl-

like away, in
to another room.

in this new room,
lit only by

my fingertips,
i held girl-like

to my mouth, un
til she entered

me. and we: child
and woman loved

each other un
disturbed.

one size ain't all

lemme tellya
how it is to be a
coffeecinammon
pecandarkoak
deepfudge mocho
cocoa colored woman
in need of some pantee-hose,
lip-o-stick, or same i-shaa-dough
and you enter one of them one size fits
kinda stores and them flu-rest-scents
hit your eyes, olive and ash your skin
tryin to make you blend, but you ain't
goin for the shine. you stomp
on to sock and stocking section first.
thin cardboard cut-out legs flex
and point down at you. but you're
poised and quiet, check the aisle
for possible re-inforce-ments. like what
have your girlfriends been wearin?
but you've been alone before.
you hunt your color in the mix
of off-black and smokey taupe,
in the tangle of natural beige
and florida suntan, in the haze of
misty fleshtone and nifty wildrice,
in the sparkle of new true brown,
warmth of tropical walnut. you hope
check the aisle again. open new
true brown on the sly,

one size ain't all

pull a leg out, put your hand through,
see if it goes with any true browns
you know. it doesn't. smokey taupe's
burnt out. you hate florida.
ain't a thing wild 'bout that there rice.
walnuts are too hard to crack.
now you're thinkin of lip-o-stick
and i-shaa-dough. you're battle weary
and hungry. cashmoney cryin in your palm.
you therefore, strategically buy
that off-black again. carry it as a lethal
weapon to that rubee-red, pee-cock blue
make-up counter again. scan the counter
for hues closest to your heart.
your heart breaks. you purchase
rubee and pee-cock. deep breathe
as the koolaid friendly sales gal
loads your goods into small white
bags. the aisle's still empty
but you know your mama will cover
your back. you march under
those flu-rest-scents again, towards exit.
swear never to sweat for these comm-odd-itties
ever again, no, never, ever
sweat odd-itties
again.

a girl and her doll

whatya want outta me?
i'm not comin outta the closet.
you people don't make it
easy. i'm thirteen. she's older,
neat, clean, pretty. i just,
i don't know, just want
to hold her, hold a woman
without being called a weird
name. without goin home
all beat up. like, what do you
want me to say, say i'm a demon
child, say i'm drugged.
are those pains better. no.
i go with barbie. not like
the other girls, or the boys.
i just go with her real quiet.
in my room. i got nothin
but barbie stuff. i like
her clothes. her hair.
i don't know, i just be
with her. normal for me
and barbie to be in the closet
together, we're kind of like
the same. lonely girls
with too many people

a girl and her doll

pointing at us. barbie's
are the first girl lips
i've kissed, the first girl lips
i've claimed as mine.
so what's all this, you gonna
write about me and her, or
what?

shelter

i entered the male,
found his wood,
and built myself
a home.

i entered the female
found her wood,
and built myself
a fire.

divorce

tumbling from a plane
by disaster or desire, thirty seconds
falling, almost flying, almost free.
descent increases. space tightens.
you feel sucked in. first pull:
parachute doesn't respond.
second pull: as unresponsive as first.
you hunt air for wings: bird, or divine.
third pull: parachute opens, flinging
you up by your armpits, sweeping
you right then left. ground becomes clearer.
you maneuver you entire being away
from jagged rocks: bold bits of stubbornness
which will pull you apart. somewhere you land.
touch your face for scars. kiss earth
and old family pictures you hold in a
chest pocket. those who have fallen
before pat you on your back,
wish you a safe drive home.

abide #1

my tongue's
in need
of your
moist
center.

its tip
a raven
nous
flower
aching
in its
dry pink
ness.

abide #2

in the
canoe
of your
lips

i'll
settle
my hips
and rock

in the
rise
of your
moons

a man and his doll

barbie made me do it.
i confess. i've known of
barbies' pectorals and gluteals
for ten years, or more.
i'm fixated gentlemen. i'm sure
you know what i mean. i mean
this: i'm in the toy store looking
for a gift for a friend's daughter
and i figure a doll. right. you
have a girl and the girl has dolls.
i enter the doll section and all
the baby dolls appear dead,
naked, bottle rubberband around
the wrist, toes rigg-a-morfied
and cold. i move to the adult doll
section. there's barbie. hair
tickling her gluteals, pecs poppin out
of the box, gluteals as firm and round
as any cannon projectile i've ever laid
my hands on, and those eyes that
get right on you, hold you there
almost at groin level. you know
what i'm saying. i'm saying i was
amazed. i touched the box, opened
the thin, pink lid, pulled her out by
her long hair, grabbed her by that
thin waist and my thumb landed
there, in the middle and i

a man and his doll

swear she's wethot. weird how they
make toys these days.
without thinking of who i am
or where i was, innocently, i squeezed her
into my pants pocket, the left one
because when my boomerang's
on guard, it bends to the left.
you guys know what i'm saying?
this here's it, without erasure or glorification.
i'm saying i paid for barbie.
took her un-gift-wrapped.
in the taxi i stretched her
across my thigh. the left thigh.
i knew i was about to do wrong.
unspeakable. hell i was hooked.
i loved barbie, loved loving barbie.
i would have to buy my friend's
daughter another gift. jacks
or pick-up sticks. or a good solid monopoly
game. i wouldn't dare look at any
other doll after barbie, no sir.
i took her under my briefcase several
times, my whole hand swallowing her body.
my left thumb holding down her face.

barbie out of the box

i said to ken, ken i said
i'm sick of it, sick to the ends
of my total hair, to the very last
curl ken, ken sick to the very end
of the curl where it hooks and dips
into my hip joint. i wanted to move him.
ken sick to the very end where the curl
splits in two and one splits in my hip joint
and the other split's you know where.
and don't stand there in that cheap suit
and plastic shoes with idiot laces, ken,
don't stand there with that constipated
buster brown smile glued on your face
and your arms held in full zombie attack.
ken, ken it's making me crazy. i don't understand
it anymore. not in this day and age. ken a fly
has more rise. ken, what are you. when's the last time
you really asked yourself that simple question?
what are you ken? a hard body without plumbing?
i've been asking that about you all the time, from
the very first day ken. remember the very first day?
the promise ken. the great mattel promise.
they racked you there next to me. remember ken,
the two of us, there, hot babes under those florescents:
me a bit dizzy from that new hairdo implant. you
breathless from the long stay in your male mold.
the promise ken. the heat of it. once the paint of my eyes
dried, and my neck settled in, i looked you over.
you couldn't see me, they were still playing with

barbie out of the box

the shape and color of your eyes,. but i looked you
over good kenneth: head to toe, toe to
middle, middle to head, middle to middle. the promise
ken. i thought it was some sort of special, slow rising,
non-light reacting male latex they used on you
down there ken. i kept watching all through the night,
into the dawn when your hair mold had settle in
and your eyes were painted wide and blue,
watched as they dressed us: you in
gray top hat, gray and black pin-striped
tails, me in white satin and a halo of pearls, a bouquet
of tiny white, silk flowers wrapped around my right
wrist. it was 1965 ken. i wanted to pull on your bowtie,
perhaps the trick was in the bowtie, somewhere
in the knot. they boxed us together, in a glittering
white and pink box, pictures of flowers and bells
everywhere. the ride from the rack to the shelf
was long and bumpy. you were quiet.
but even in veil i shamelessly watched your center,
then your hands, thinking the thoughts i had heard
the mattel men speak: how maybe it would itch and grow,
and you'd take it in your hand like a happy baby boy,
and giggle over me, or how it will burst from the box
and rest in my hair, move to my ear, my neck.
the mattel men laughed loud about it and you ken.
i believed their powers and yours, but your hands
remain open and empty ken, same as you middle ken,
same as your smile.

VOWS

man if you laugh
or sing in your sleep
i'll marry you,

lay in the underbelly
of your sex where
little boys hidden

from you and war
live with kites
and caterpillars.

i'll rub my breasts
into your thighs,
release my little girls,

their bows and braids
tickling your little boys
cheeks. i'll marry you,

in the curves
of these children,
oil our skin with their

anxious tongues,
until one morning,
when we grow blind

and very stiff, drop
to our knees, crawl into
their damp, empty space.

why i like being called baby
(for: TDH)

even in this postmodern,
post-re-constructionist,
de-constructionist, radical
re-defined-feminist, womanist
masculinist, re-inscribed male
agendas, multicultural contexturalizations,
intertextual discourse, narratization,
discursive signifying, poly paradigmatic
meta materiality methodologies,
object, subject, code, kind of reflective;

there is a pulsing,
timed, swirling like a comet
at the end of my midnight
tip, which when stroked, cuddled,
whispered to prettily,
coos and lays me flat

out.

peace #2

(from a piece of conversation
 i overheard on a nyc train)

and the old black man said,
-what you gonna lose
by bein nice. shit. your
life? hell you been here
before. you be here agin.
now be nice. get up!-

about the poet:

safiya henderson-holmes, is also a mother and a physiotherapist, and presently ass't professor in the creative writing program of syracuse university. her first book of poems, *madness and a bit of hope* won the poetry society of america's william carlos williams award. *daily bread* is her second book.

notes:

food: based on the shooting death of a 15 year old african-american female by an adult female korean store owner in los angeles. the incident took place a few weeks before the rodney king uprisings in los angeles. this shooting was on the store's videotape, the videotape was shown in court. the store owner was found not guilty.

force: based on the rodney king verdict in los angeles and an imagined female juror and her own very real oppression.

life: based on the rodney king uprisings and the imagined voice of reginald denny: the truck driver who was pulled from his truck, beaten by black men and then rescued and brought to the hospital by black men.

love: based on the rodney king uprisings and the imagined voice of one of the black men accused of beating truck driver reginald denny.

speculations: based on the situations surrounding the wanda webb holloway case: the mother who wanted her daughter on the highschool cheerleading squad badly enough to plot the killing of a competitor's mother.

a news note: based on moments in the life of cedric sandiford's and imagined news 'note' to comment on the 'flash in the pants' life the media gives to some very important aspects of our world.

where to look
for black love: a response to the controversial and popular book; "the blackman's guide to understanding the blackwoman," by

name
#129,002 and
counting: the number and phrase; "129,002 and counting":was taken from the village voice article, "129,001 and counting." by larry kramer. village voice, 12/10/91.

*the quote which opens poems is from the short story, "sonny's blues" by james baldwin.

OHIO UNIVERSITY LIBRARY
Please return this book as soon as you have
finished with it. In order to avoid a fine it must
 turned by the latest dat